THE CRAFTS OF FLORIDA'S FIRST PEOPLE

Robin C. Brown

D1413533

PINEAPPLE PRESS, INC.
SARASOTA, FLORIDA

143097

This book is dedicated to my grandchildren, Claire,
Emily, Frances, Elizabeth, Robin, Sarah, and Margaret, with love

Inquiries should be addressed to:
Pineapple Press, Inc.
P.O. Box 3889
Sarasota, Florida 34230

www.pineapplepress.com

Library of Congress Cataloging-in-Publication Data

Brown, Robin C., 1934–.
The crafts of Florida's first people / Robin C. Brown.
        p. cm.
Summary: Provides instructions for craft projects based on the work of the
Calusa and other early Florida Indians.
Includes bibliographical references.
    ISBN 978-1-56164-282-3 (pbk. : alk. paper)
1. Handicraft—Juvenile literature. 2. Calusa Indians—Juvenile literature. 3.
Indians of North America—Florida—Juvenile literature.
[1. Handicraft. 2. Calusa Indians. 3. Indians of North America—Florida. 4.
Prehistoric
peoples.] I. Title.

TT160.B854 2003
745.4'49759—dc21   2003010984

First Edition
10 9 8 7 6 5 4 3 2

Design by Shé Hicks
Printed in the United States of America

A NOTE TO PARENTS AND TEACHERS

The story of Florida's prehistoric people is rapidly coming to light. Archaeologists working on projects all over the state are putting together the fascinating tale of the first 12,000 years of human occupation of Florida. Florida people once hunted elephants with spears. For thousands of years they buried their dead under water. Some 8,000-year-old human skulls actually contain preserved brains.

Along with the broad picture, thousands of details of everyday living are emerging. But almost all this information is published in academic journals, and very little has been written for school-age children. Yet these young people are hungry to know how ancient Florida Indians lived and are eager to try the things that allowed them to survive in prehistoric Florida.

This book is written for young people ages ten years and up. Some of the projects require little adult help, and some, like firing pottery, require a lot. Cautions are included for projects that employ fire (making fire, firing pottery), might be injurious (traps and darts), or suggest using poisonous materials (pokeberry juice for paints). The naturally occurring materials needed for some of the crafts may not be locally available, and workable substitutes are noted where appropriate.

To make the projects more meaningful and more fun, a bit of Florida archaeology and ancient history is presented alongside the craft instructions. If the interest of the reader-craftsman is aroused, sources for additional information are listed at the end.

FOR YOUR SAFETY

Some of the activities in this book involve sharp objects, potentially harmful substances, and fire. Follow all necessary safety precautions. All of the activities in this book should be undertaken with the supervision of a qualified adult. Neither the author nor the publisher will assume responsibility for accidents or injuries that occur while engaging in any of the activities outlined in this book.

CONTENTS

INTRODUCTION

HOW I LEARNED ABOUT FLORIDA INDIANS

In May of 1990 I sat at a table covered with spotless white paper, gazing at a bunch of twisted black string. The room, buried on the lowest floor of the Florida Museum of Natural History, had no windows. Outside, students at the University of Florida were throwing Frisbees in the late spring sunshine. But the stuff I was looking at was too precious to expose to sunlight. The pieces of netting before me were probably 1,000 years old, made by a vanished tribe of Florida Indians known as Calusa. The Calusa were skilled at fishing, and this brittle net once caught boatloads of mullet.

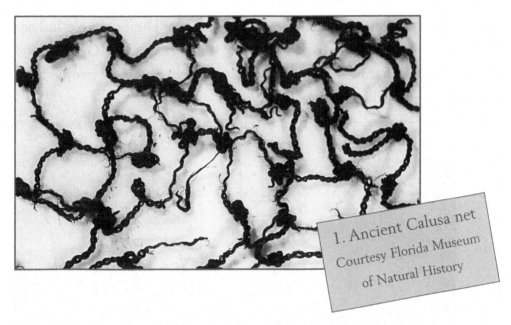

I had come to the museum at the invitation of Dr. Bill Marquardt who was studying the Calusa Indians, ancient people who once lived along Florida's lower Gulf coast. Bill knew that a book about the first people to live in Florida was needed and he had asked me to write it. He helped me every step of the way and four years later *Florida's First People* was published. I am very grateful to Bill.

While at the museum I took close-up pictures of the net and read about its history. I learned that it had been made of palm leaves. But a lot of questions remained, questions that I had been asking since I began my book. How hard was it to make a net? How long did it take? How strong was it? No one seemed to know.

The same sort of questions cropped up again and again as I tried to tell about the things Florida Indians had to be able to make in order to survive. What did their cloth feel like? Can you really bake clay pots in an open fire? And how do you start the fire in the first place?

There were people living in Florida for 12,000 years before Columbus got here. These people lived all over the state, and there were at least 100,000 of them—maybe a lot more—here in 1492. During those 12,000 years, the first Indians learned a lot about what it takes to live in Florida. But these first Florida people are gone now. The last true Florida Indian died 200 years ago. The Seminole Indians who live in Florida today came to Florida from Georgia and Alabama because of huge changes brought about by people from Europe settling in the New World.

2. Model of a Calusa village
Courtesy Florida Museum of Natural History

Since none of the first Florida people are left to answer my questions, I decided to see if I could make some of the things they used. I would learn how strong their cord was by making it (and breaking it, too), how many clay pots cracked in the fire, and just how hard it was to make fire without matches. Some things turned out to be easier than I thought they would be and some were harder. But always the crafts were fun to do, and it was neat to know how Florida's first people—people just like you and me—made the things they used during the first 12,000 years of Florida human history.

Today the museums are collecting objects, but tomorrow it will be technology. It will then be necessary to take a new approach, for you can't save practical knowledge by putting it in a museum storeroom. You must pass it on. The day will come.

—Thomas Johansen, Founder of the Institute for Prehistoric Technology in Sweden

1. CORD, STRING, AND ROPE

Florida's first people had no nails, no screws, no sticky tape, and no good glue, so they used string and rope to hold things together. They truly tied their world together. Fiber is the stuff that you need to make thread, string, cord, and rope, and you need a lot of it.

Archaeologists study people of long ago by looking carefully at the things these people left behind. Archaeologists know for sure that early Florida Indians used the leaves of the sabal or cabbage palm for thread, cord, and rope because they have found ancient ropes, nets, and cloth, all made of palm fiber. The two best finds of these materials are Windover, near the Kennedy Space Center, and Marco Island on the Gulf of Mexico, near Naples.

Florida's Indians ate a lot of fish. They caught fish using cord with hooks made of bone. They tied the cord into fishing nets. Canoes, which they made by burning out the inside of pine logs, were used for fishing and for getting around in Florida. Rope was needed to tie up canoes.

3. An archaeologist at work

MAKING PALM LEAF CORD

I decided to start my "how did they make?" trials by making cord from the leaves of the sabal palm. I got help from Dr. Bill Payne, a botanist who taught me to twist up the fiber so that it didn't come apart. His wife, June, is an expert on spinning and weaving, and she taught me the right names for the things that I was doing. This is what I learned about plying cord:

There are threadlike tan-colored fibers 10 to 30 inches long hanging from the fan-shaped leaves of the sabal palm. Gather a bunch of these fibers from big palm leaves. Making the fibers into cord is called **plying.** Take a bundle of six to eight fibers and fold the bundle in half. At the fold, twist the fibers together and loop them over a fixed post to steady them as you work. A nail hammered into a board makes a good post.

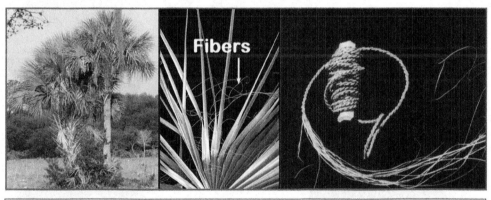

4. Sabal palm   Leaf fibers   Cord from sabal palm

5. Looping the bundle of fibers

When you have the fiber bundle looped over the post, moisten the fingers of both hands. Holding one bundle in each hand, pull gently against the post and twist the fiber bundles using the thumb and first finger. Twist with both hands and twist both bundles in the same direction as shown in picture 6. While still holding the bundles, cross your hands over each other, wrapping the two twisted bundles together in the *opposite* direction from the direction of the twist. This twisting and wrapping keeps the cord that you have made from

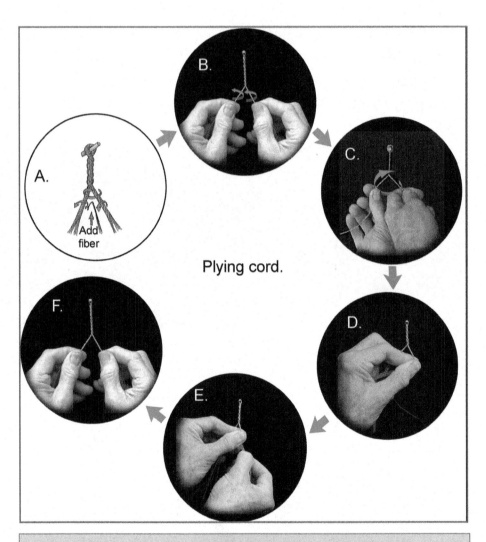

Plying cord.

6. Plying cord

CORD, STRING, AND ROPE

coming untwisted when you let go. As you continue plying, you will begin to run out of fibers. When this happens, add one or two more fibers, twisting them into the cord as shown. Snip off the ends of the fibers that are left sticking out of your cord.

For a strong neatly made cord, add small amounts of fiber often. Fibers that are long make plying easier because you don't have to add more fibers as often. When the cord is about two feet long, you can take it off the post. I tried holding the cord in my teeth as I plied; this works, but causes drooling. Looping the cord around a toe also works, but leads to toe cramps. The best way is to roll the cord up on a stick. Hold the stick down with a rock or your foot. As you make more cord, wrap the cord on the stick. Two-ply cord can be made into four-ply rope by twisting and wrapping in directions opposite to the first plying as shown in picture 7.

7. Plying two-ply cord into four ply

You can also split the green sabal palm leaf itself into narrow strips—they must be narrower than a pencil lead—and ply them into cord.

PALM TRUNK FIBER CORD

Archaeologists have found very old cord and cloth in South America that was made from cotton and from llama wool. I had read that some Indians in North America made a sort of yarn from opossum hair, but it seemed to me that you would have to shave an awful lot of opossums to get enough hair to make much yarn. I wondered whether there was any soft fiber like cotton or fur that Florida's natives might have used. To my surprise, I found there was—right there on the trunk of the sabal palm. This stuff is much like cotton and is even a bit like fur. Where the leaf stem joins the trunk of the sabal palm, there is an opening that contains a reddish fiber that is fairly soft. It can be plied into very nice yarn for weaving and made into strong rope. Here's how:

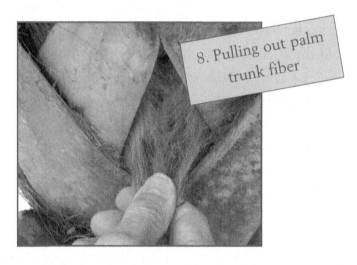

8. Pulling out palm trunk fiber

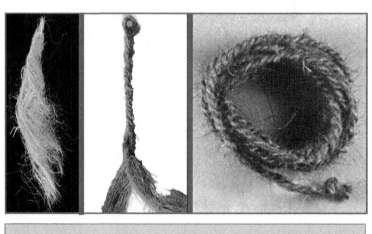

| 9. Palm "fur" | Plying | Cord from palm "fur" |

Find a sabal palm that has the leaf stems still attached to the trunk and pull this reddish palm "fur" out from about ten of these openings. Stretch the fibers out (a comb helps to do this) and ply them into cord. The fur is a little harder to ply because the fibers are short and you will have to add bunches of fibers more often than you did when using leaf fibers. If you make the two-ply cord into four-ply rope, you will have a soft rope that is surprisingly strong.

ROPE FROM SPANISH MOSS

The Spanish moss that hangs from Florida trees like long gray beards makes wonderful rope.

Spanish moss is hard to work with when fresh, but when the gray-green outer covering of the fibers is removed, the black, shiny inner fiber can be plied into strong rope.

The outer green covering can be rotted away by placing a large bundle of green moss under water for two or three weeks. This is process called retting. After retting, only the curly black fiber is left.

10. Spanish moss

Gather an armful of Spanish moss and put it under water. A pond is a good place, but you can use a ten gallon bucket. Weight the moss down with rocks. Check the moss every week and when all of it has

11. Spanish moss before retting

After retting

turned black, take it out and wash it off.. To make it into rope, pull out this tough, black fiber into a strand about ⅜ inch in diameter, and ply it just as you did the palm fiber.

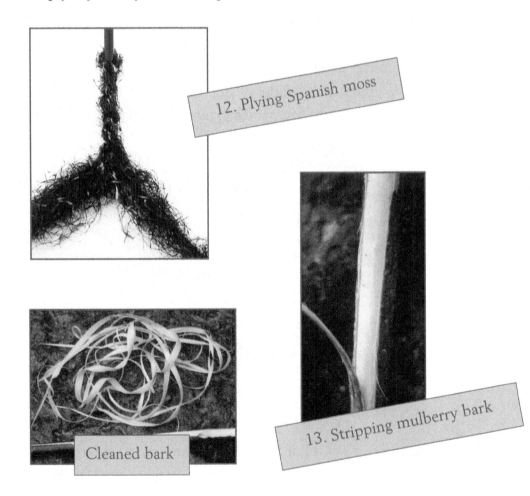

12. Plying Spanish moss

Cleaned bark

13. Stripping mulberry bark

BARK CORD

All over the world people have made the inner bark of trees into a very strong cord. Archaeologists haven't yet found traces of bark cord made by Florida's natives, but bark cord may turn up yet.

Good cord-making bark comes from willow, mulberry, poplar, and basswood trees. Use a limb that doesn't have many branches. Peel the bark in long strips and scrape and wash off the thin outer bark. Split the clean, wet, inner bark into strips about the width of a pencil lead and ply

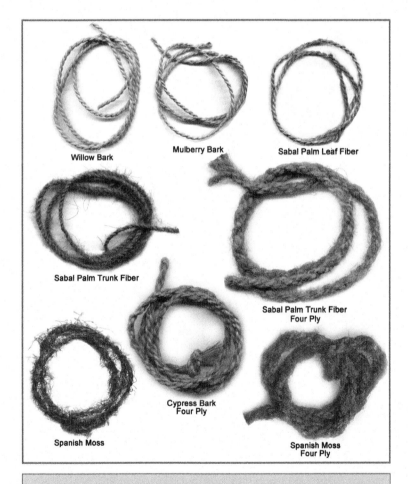

14. Cords from various Florida fibers

them into cord while still wet. Bark cord gets a little stiff when it dries, but is *really* strong.

IF YOU CAN'T GO NATURAL...

If you can't use any of the fibers used by Florida Indians, many craft stores sell a palm fiber called raffia, which you can ply into pretty good cord.

---

2. WEAVING

A few years back I was in Tallahassee sitting across from Dr. Glen Doran in his lab at Florida State University. Every table in the lab was covered with rows of bones. Glen is one of the archaeologists who uncovered the 8,000-year-old remains of people who lived near what is today Titusville. On the bottom of a shallow pond, buried in black muck, the archaeologist found objects and bones that were almost perfectly preserved—cloth that was wrapped around the bodies, and, most amazingly, skulls that still contained human brain. The site, which is now world famous, is named Windover.

Glen, who is one of the most generous people I know, talked with me for hours about Windover. He told me that archaeologists who study the fiber-craft of ancient people believe that the first people who came into Florida 12,000 years ago already knew how to weave cloth and mats and make baskets. But they had to learn what Florida plants were best for each of these things. At Windover, Glen described finding finely made cloth (some of it had 24 threads to the inch!) that was woven by Florida people 8,000 years ago. Like their cord and rope, the fiber came from the leaves of the sabal palm.

By this time I was pretty good at plying fiber into cord so I decided to see how hard it would be to weave my cord into cloth. Here is a way to build a simple loom and weave cloth.

15. Woven cloth from Windover site
Courtesy Dr. Glen Doran

First, make about 15 feet of palm leaf cord that is about $\frac{1}{16}$ inch in diameter. This will be the **warp**—the cords that run up and down the loom that you will weave on. You will then need another 15 feet of cord to be woven into the warp cords. This is called the **weft**. Weft cords are best made from that reddish palm fur and it's okay if they are thicker and fuzzier than the warp.

MAKE YOUR LOOM

1. Choose a Y-shaped branch. The thickest part of the branch that is the base of the Y, should be ½ to ¾ inch in diameter and about 24 inches long. The arms of the Y should be about 20 inches long.

2. Make two cross pieces and notch them where they will cross the arms of the Y as shown in picture 16A. The cross pieces should be about 16 inches apart.

Cut eight small notches in the upper and lower cross pieces as shown. If you use all of the notches, you will have 16 warp cords. The notches will keep these cords in place. Bind the cross pieces to the Y frame with some of the warp cord you have made as shown in picture 16B.

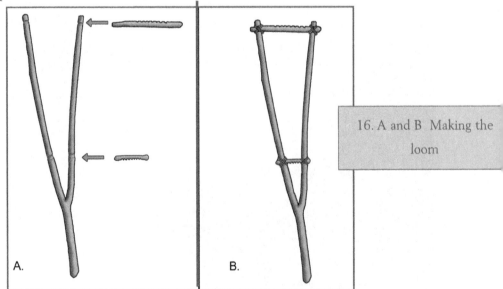

16. A and B Making the loom

A.

B.

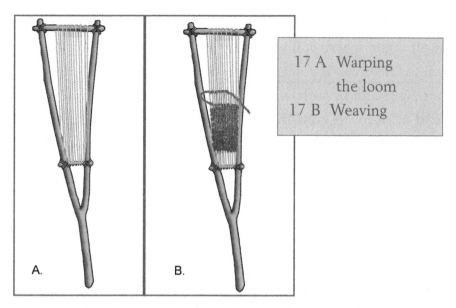

17 A Warping
      the loom
17 B Weaving

A.

B.

WARP YOUR LOOM

Putting the warp cords on the loom is called warping: Tie one end of the warp cord to the bottom crosspiece on the left side and loop the warp cord over the cross pieces as shown in picture 17A. Each loop gives you two warp cords. You can have as many as 16 warp cords, but fewer are okay. Each cord should be pulled snug but not tightly stretched. When the warp is in place, tie off the cord to the right side of the bottom cross piece.

WEAVING

You are now ready to start weaving. Stick the base of the Y into the ground to hold the loom still while you work. Start from the left side, about three inches up from the bottom cross piece and pass the weft cord over and under the warp cords as shown in picture 17B. You can usually weave through four or five warp cords and still be able to pull the rest of the weft through. If your warp and weft cords are smooth, you may be able to weave over and under as many as 16 warps at one time. At the beginning of the weaving you will have a lot of weft cord to pull through the warp. After each pass through all the warp cords, pull the weft snug where it loops around the warp and pack the weft down with the blunt edge of a plastic knife (the Indians used a smooth piece of bone). When you start the second row, pass the weft under where you went over and over where you went under on the first row. If you run out of weft and need to add more, take a new length of weft cord and overlap it about ½ inch with the end of the weft cord that ran out and keep weaving. When you have made as long a weaving as you want, cut the warp threads where they loop over the bottom crosspiece and tie off each pair as shown in picture 18. Do the same for the top and the weaving won't come undone.

Here are some weaves that I did on a simple loom like the one shown. The cloth is coarse and pretty scratchy. I think the Windover weavers had more practice and skill than I had.

18. Weaving tied off

19. Weaving done on the simple loom

Palm leaf warp and trunk fiber weft

Trunk fiber warp and weft

3. BASKET MAKING

As far as we can tell, all of Florida's first people did a lot of gathering. They picked or picked up things like acorns, hickory nuts, berries, and roots. And from the seashores they gathered oysters, clams, and other shellfish that were good to eat. If you don't have paper, plastic, or metal, baskets are the answer for bringing what you have gathered home. Unfortunately, baskets don't last very long when buried in the ground and only a few basket remains have been found by archaeologists in Florida. Guess where? At Windover, of course.

20. Making a basket using palmetto stems

21. Basket being uncovered from Windover muck

Baskets must have been used a lot, and there is some great basket-making stuff in Florida. My friend Dick Workman is a skilled basket maker and has used just about every basket-making material that Florida has to offer. Dick taught me basket making. My first one was pretty poor: it would hold grapefruit, but anything smaller would fall through the gaps in the weaving. Dick was patient and my baskets got better—though none were as good as his. I started making baskets from the stems of palmettos because palmettos grow just about everywhere in Florida, and the stems are long, straight, and easy to split.

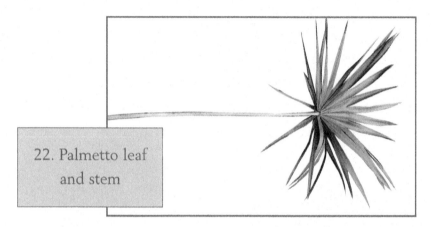

22. Palmetto leaf and stem

Here's how:

1. Cut about 20 stems. Choose green stems that are at least two feet long. Scrape off the saw edge on both sides, and trim them all to two feet. Use a knife, and be careful.

2. You will be splitting the stem into what basket makers call splints. If you look at the cut end of a palmetto stem, you will see that it is shaped like the letter D.

Starting at the small end of the stem (closest to where the leaf was), split a stem into halves as shown in picture 23. As you split, if one half of the split stem gets thicker than the other, put your thumb on the thick side, right where the stem is splitting, and bend that side more sharply. When you have split all the stems into halves, go on to split the flat half again as shown in picture 23.

Now split the splint that has the flat, green, shiny side in two as shown in the picture. Eight of these splints with the green side facing out will be used for the basket's ribs. They should be about $1/16$ inch thick and about ¼ inch wide. You will need three or four more ribs that will be added as the basket gets bigger. The

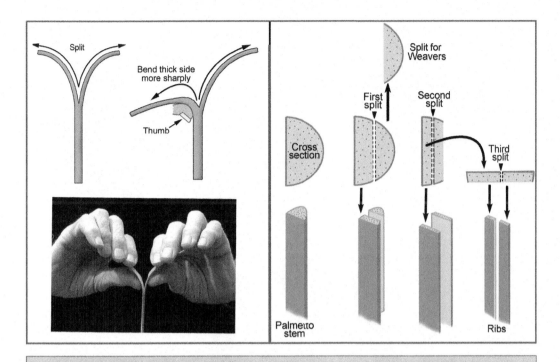

23. Splitting a palmetto stem

unused splints will be further split to make the weavers. Weavers are splints that will be woven into the ribs. Make the weavers by splitting the rest of the D-shaped part of the stems into halves and then into quarters. Split a few even finer. All the splints should be kept wet until they are used so that they will stay easy to bend. Coil them in a bucket of water.

To weave the basket:

3. Take two groups of four ribs and cross them in the middle. Be sure the shiny green parts are all facing down—this will be the outside of the basket. With the thinnest weaver that you split, begin passing it over and under the groups of four ribs (picture 24).

4. After a row or two, begin going over and under two ribs (picture 25).

5. After three or four more rows, go over and under each rib (picture 26). When you come to the end of a weaver, tuck it neatly along a rib into the weaving you have already done. Start another weaver by tucking in the end in the same way. Pointing the end of the weaver helps.

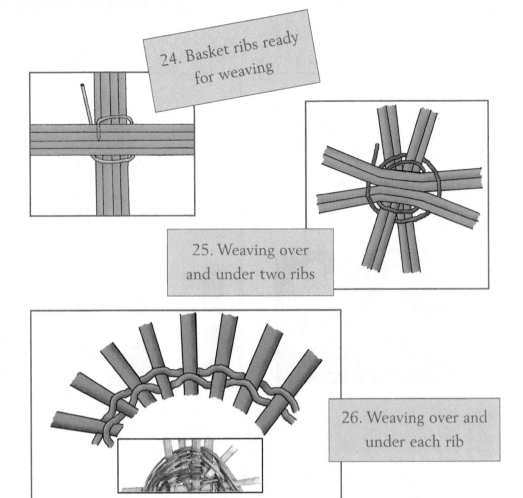

24. Basket ribs ready for weaving

25. Weaving over and under two ribs

26. Weaving over and under each rib

6. For the weave to come out right, there must be an odd number of ribs. So cut one of your extra ribs in two (making two 12 inch ribs) and point one end. Stick a 12-inch rib into the weave to make another rib; choose a place where there is a gap. This makes nine ribs so each row of weaving will come out right. As the bottom of the basket gets bigger, you will need to add more ribs, but always keep an odd number of ribs.

7. When the bottom is about five inches across, gently bend the ribs up, keeping the shiny side out. Hold the bent ribs up with a rubber band around their ends (picture 27). Start weaving upward, forming the sides of the basket. After a few rows, you can take off the rubber band. When the basket is four or five inches high, cut off the ribs so that they stick out about three inches above the last row of weaving.

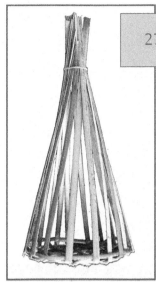

27. Ribs tied

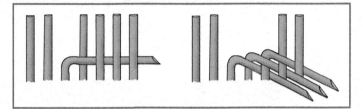

28. Beginning the rim

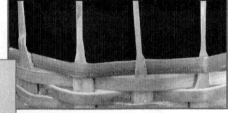

29. Ribs thinned

30. Rim, first round.

8. To make the basket's rim, take a rib and bend it to the right as shown in picture 28. If the ribs start to crack as you bend them, thin them with the knife until they bend without cracking (picture 29). Then bend the rib outside the next rib to the right and inside the next rib. Do the same with the next rib to the right of the first rib and continue around the rim. Each rib will hold down the one before it, (picture 30).

9. On the second round of rim weaving, going in the same direction, choose a rib, lift up the rib to the right of it, and poke the rib through the space created as shown in picture 31.

When you have gone around the rim for the second time, all the

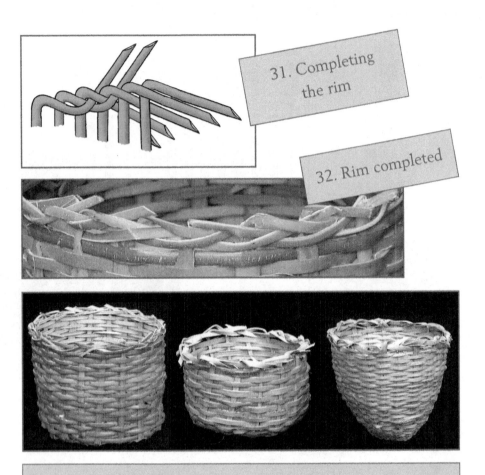

31. Completing the rim

32. Rim completed

33. Baskets made of palmetto stem

ribs will be sticking inside the basket and can be trimmed neatly (picture 32). Don't trim them too closely or they may pop out of place later when the basket dries and shrinks.

The roots of sabal palm and palmetto can also be made into good baskets. Sometimes you can find these roots that are six or eight feet long. Sabal palm roots are easiest to pull up on beaches or riverbanks where water is washing away the sand.

Palm and palmetto roots are also pushed out where land is being cleared. Pull as much of the root from the ground as you can—the longer the better. Cut it off when no more will come loose and coil it up. Soak the roots in water for two or three days and then clean off the soft outer part. What is left makes a super weaver.

34. Sabal palm with roots exposed

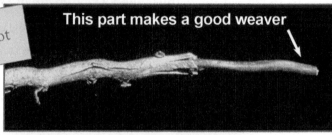

35. Close-up of sabal palm root

This part makes a good weaver

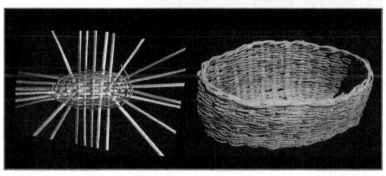

36. Baskets of palmetto stem and palmetto roots

Coil the palm root under water just as you did with the palmetto stems. You can make a handsome basket from palmetto stem ribs and palm root weavers.

IF YOU CAN'T GO NATURAL...

If you can't use the natural materials, craft stores sell basketmaking reed in several thicknesses. Be sure to keep the reed wet while using it.

4. TRAPS

When people first arrived in Florida 12,000 years ago, there were elephants and other big animals. It's great to imagine the people hunting them with spears, arrows, and knives. But much of their food was probably small animals like rabbits and raccoons that they caught in traps. Traps are really fun to make. I got plans for many kinds of traps from a great magazine called *The Bulletin of Primitive Technology* (a magazine for people who want to learn early crafts). The address is in Chapter 10. The people who write articles for this magazine like to say, "Primitive means first, *not* worst."

Remember that Florida's first people set traps to get food. But today there is plenty of food, and so there is no excuse for killing or injuring an animal.

The thing that sets off the trap is called the trigger. The bait is some kind of food that the animal you want to catch likes to eat. The bait is stuck on the trigger. Here are two traps that have triggers set so that even a tiny pull on the bait will spring the trap. I caught a rabbit (for 10 seconds until he dug his way out) with the box trap. But even if you don't catch anything, you will learn a lot from building traps:

A FIGURE FOUR TRAP

A cardboard box can be used for the trap itself. It should be square and about two feet on a side. Put a heavy board on top to add weight. The trigger looks like the number four and is made from three sticks, about ¾ inches in diameter. The sticks are cut as shown in the picture. They can be from any wood and the bark can be left on. When set just right, even a slight tug on the bait will drop the box over the animal. A piece of dry corncob with a few kernels left on is good bait for squirrels.

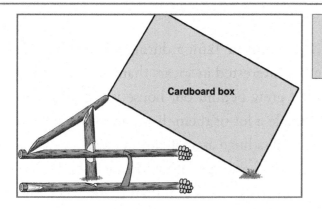

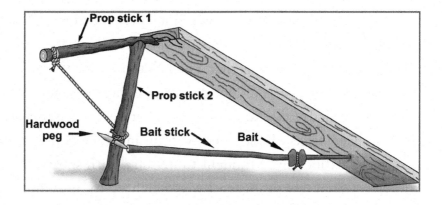

37. A figure 4 trap

38. A deadfall trap

The deadfall was built to kill by dropping a heavy rock on the animal that goes for the bait. Since our plan is not to murder small animals, use a piece of light wooden board instead of the rock—a 2 ½-foot long piece of two-by-six works well. To set, rest prop stick 1 on prop stick 2. Prop the board so that it rests right at the edge of prop stick 1. Then bring the cord around prop stick 2 and set up the bait stick. You may need to carve a small nick in the board at the point where the bait stick touches it. If the sticks are set as shown, the two prop sticks will be flipped out of the way of the falling board. A feather touch will spring this one.

5. ATLATLS

Even though I grew up in Tampa during World War II, I was always more interested in spears than guns. The pencil bamboo that grew behind our house was great spear-making material, and I made a lot of them. But I always wondered whether you could really kill a huge animal like an elephant with a spear. How could you get close enough without being trampled?

In college I was surprised to learn that there were elephants—both mammoths and mastodons—in North America as recently as 11,000 years ago. Since people entered Florida for the first time 12,000 years ago, for about 1,000 years people and elephants lived here together. Then all the elephants and all the other big Ice Age beasts of Florida—camels, horses, saber cats, and a big lion called *Felis atrox*—became extinct or disappeared. Some archaeologists think that overhunting by people caused these mass extinctions. I thought to myself, "With spears? Wow!"

So a few years ago I was delighted to meet Jim Dunbar, an archaeologist who works for the state of Florida and who was particularly interested in the time when humans and huge animals were both living here. We talked about how a man with a spear could kill an elephant. One of the important things I learned about was the atlatl (pronounced at-**lat**-ul). What is an atlatl? It is a spear-throwing stick that was invented thousands of years ago and has been used by hunters all over the world.

39A. Silified chert point likely for an atlatl. Mid-Archaic.
Found near Tampa by Dean Quigley

39. An atlatl in use
Drawing by David Meo

40. Wooden atlatl found
at Key Marco site

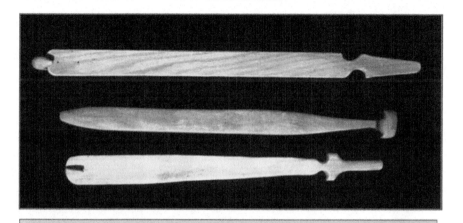

41. Three atlatls that I made

An atlatl lets you throw a spear or dart with much more power than you have if you just throw with your arm. The atlatl makes your throwing arm longer so that the tip of the atlatl that pushes the spear moves really fast. Also, the springy wood of some atlatls bends backward as the atlatl moves forward carrying the spear, and at the end of the throw, the bent atlatl straightens out and pushes the spear even harder.

The tip of the atlatl must fit neatly into the back end of the spear or dart. The fit must to be strong enough to stand the swing, yet loose enough to easily let the spear go when the atlatl tip reaches the end of its throw. The atlatl handle sometimes has one or two finger holes for a better grip. Ancient atlatls with finger holes have been found on Marco Island near Naples.

Florida's first people used different lengths of atlatls and spears. When hunting in a forest with trees and bushes close by, they used a short atlatl and short spear called a dart. Out in the open the hunter couldn't get very close to the hunted animal, so he used a long atlatl and a long spear that would go a long way.

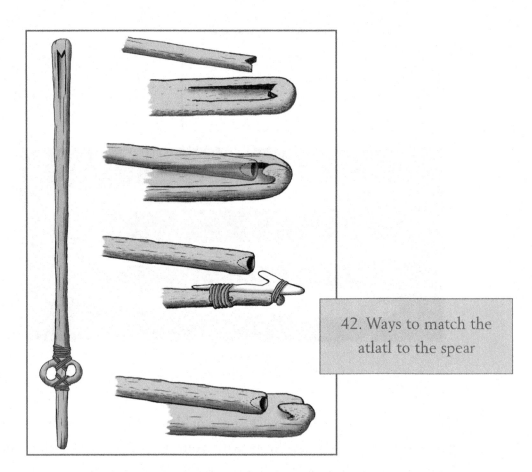

42. Ways to match the atlatl to the spear

Well, I wished that I had known all this when I was a kid, but I certainly needed to try an atlatl now. Here's how I made atlatls:

The atlatl's length and the shape of its handgrip can be made in several ways. Picture 42 shows some of the ways that the tip of the atlatl can fit into the back end of the spear.

1. Atlatls can be made from almost any wood. Willow is a good choice. Willow grows at the edges of streams and lakes all over Florida and the wood carves easily. Make the atlatl from a freshly cut limb—this will make carving much easier. It should be about 1 ½ inches in diameter at the handle end. The spur that carries the spear on one end of the atlatl can be made from a small branch that is shaped as shown in the picture. The length should be about 14 inches.

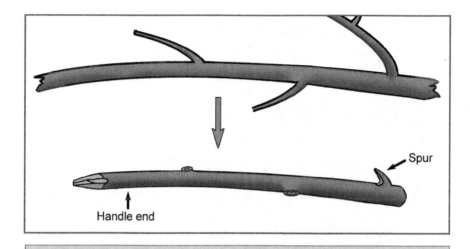

43. Making an atlatl

2. Spears or darts are made like arrows. A good stuff to use is bamboo that is ⅜ to ¾ inch-diameter. Use straight bamboo and make the spear about 3 feet in length. The big end of the spear will be the back end. If you are using bamboo, the spur of the atlatl will fit into the hollow bamboo at this end. Cut the bamboo so that a joint is about ¾ inch from the large (rear) end of the spear and a joint is about 1 ½ inches from the small (front) end.

If you can't get bamboo, cut a 3-foot length of green sabal palm leaf stem. Cut off the sharp edges and round it to about ½ inch in diameter. Sabal palm stems have a slight curve and this can be fixed by bending the stem firmly in the opposite direction until it is straight, then weighting the stem to keep it flat for about three days until it dries. Straight branches from willow and poplar also make good spears. Carve the front end to a point and cut a cone-shaped hole in the back end of the spear as shown in picture 44.

3. Three feathers must be glued to the rear end of the spear. The feathers help keep the spear going straight with the point first. Putting feathers on the spear is called **fletching**. Use scissors to cut three pieces of turkey or other large feather about 1 ½ inches wide by 3 inches long. Cut the feather so that the rib (which goes down the center of the feather) stays with the piece you are going to use. The rib is the part of

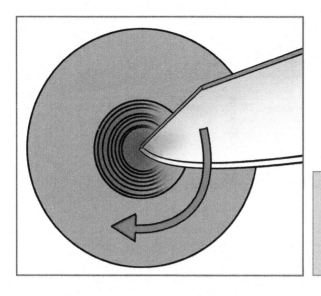

44. Cutting a hole in the back end of a spear

IF YOU CAN'T GO NATURAL...

If you can't find natural material for your spear, buy a ⅜-inch wooden dowel from the hardware store, cut it to three feet in length, and carve it as described above.

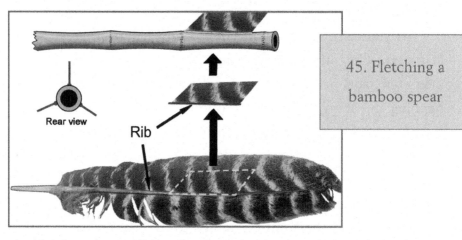

Rear view

Rib

45. Fletching a bamboo spear

the feather that will be glued to the spear. Glue each feather to the spear as shown in picture 45.

4. If you are using bamboo for your spear, make a point from sharpened hard wood like oak or hickory. Carve the point so you can stick the rear end of the point into the hollow bamboo at the

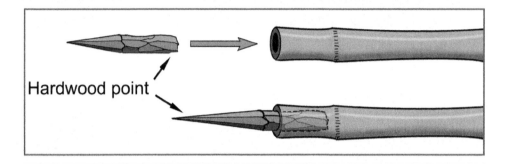

Hardwood point

46. Making the point

front end of the spear. Squirt some white glue into the hole in the bamboo before you put the point in place. Wait a day before using the spear to be sure the glue is dry.

Be careful! Have everyone stand behind you when you throw. With an atlatl, you get power a long time before you get accuracy. We drove a flint spear point one inch into a palm tree and a dart with a hardwood point shattered our screen door.

If you are righthanded, hold the atlatl in the right hand and the

47. Using the atlatl

Drawing by David Meo

35

spear in the left as shown in the drawing (picture 47). Stick the spur on the tip of the atlatl into the hole or the notch on the back end of the spear. Swing the atlatl in a wide arc over your head and let go your hold on the spear about halfway through the swing. Moving forward by one long step as you throw adds more force to the spear. Practice until your throw is both strong and accurate. Long spears take a stronger arm to throw and they go farther than short darts.

6. PAINTS

I t's April 1896. A group of workers sloshes around in muck that is often above their boots. Some are lifting buckets of water from the mucky pond and pouring it into a wooden trough that carries it away. The heat is intense and the humidity is high. To make matters worse, swarms of mosquitoes and sand flies are constantly biting. Despite the awful working conditions, the archaeologist in charge, whose name is Frank Cushing, can't believe the things that his men are

48. The Key Marco site in 1896
Courtesy Smithsonian Institutions, National Anthropological Archives

finding. Not just pottery and stone, but things carved from wood and bone, together with fiber, cord, nets, and rope are all coming out of this bad-smelling muck. This was the famous Key Marco site. It is on the Gulf of Mexico near Naples, and today it is called Marco Island.

Among Cushing's finds were several life-sized wooden masks. The masks had been carved and painted by the Calusa Indians many hundreds of years before. To everyone's surprise, the paint was still stuck to the masks and the colors were still bright. Cushing was sure that the Indians wore the masks at very special times, like when they prayed to their gods. Only a few of these masks still exist, and the paint has faded away with time, but Cushing had a good artist on his team, and the artist made paintings of the masks right after they came out of the muck.

49. Painted wooden masks from Key Marco site
Courtesy Smithsonian Institutions, National Anthropological Archives

I asked several Florida archaeologists about the masks. None of the archaeologists that I asked had any idea what the paint was made of or why it stuck so well to the masks. Cushing wrote a famous paper on the Key Marco finds, and in it he described the paint as "gum-like." After a lot of thought and tries that didn't work, I hit on the milky sap of trees in the fig family to bind my paint. The paint made from this sap—called latex— worked beautifully; the paint made with latex stuck tightly to the wood and would not wash or rub off. There is no proof that latex was the paint base used by the Calusa, but on Marco Island there were trees that could have been tapped for latex sap, and I'll bet they were.

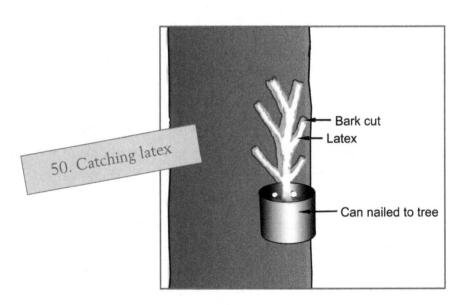

50. Catching latex

Bark cut
Latex
Can nailed to tree

IF YOU CAN'T GO NATURAL...

If you can't find the right tree for latex, white glue mixed two parts glue to one part water makes a good paint base.

In Florida, the latex that makes the paint stick comes from trees in the *ficus* family. Some of these trees are fig, banyan, rubber tree, and strangler fig. If you cut a strip of bark from one of these trees, the sticky white latex will slowly drip out and can be caught in a can fixed to the tree. The picture shows how.

Catch the drip in the can until you have one or two ounces of latex. This is the base for your paint.

I was surprised to find that you can make really good paint colors from things like colored clay, charcoal, powdered shell, and plant juices. There are colored clays in Florida that can be used to color the paints you make. We know that Florida Indians used colored clay mixed with fat to paint their bodies. Red clay, found mostly in the northern half of Florida, makes a red-brown paint and clays that are yellowish-brown, bluish, and greenish are scattered over the state. To mix with the latex, the colored clays must be powdered. Put down several sheets of newspaper to catch the powder and set a flat stone on the newspaper. Rub a piece of dried clay on the stone and catch the powdered clay on the paper. Pour the powder into a small jar (a baby food jar is the right size).

IF YOU CAN'T GO NATURAL...

I think the Calusa used something like powdered shell for white paint, but shell is hard to powder. Stuff much like shell powder called lime is sold at garden shops and makes a good white. Mix a little black paint with white paint to get a gray.

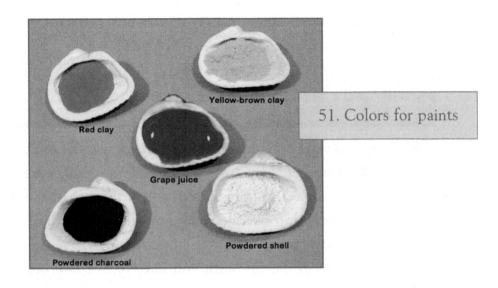

Red clay

Yellow-brown clay

Grape juice

Powdered charcoal

Powdered shell

Black paint can be made using powdered charcoal. Scrape the burned parts of sticks from an old fire on a stone as you did with the clay and save the black powder.

Plant juices make good purples and reds. Pokeberry juice is a great deep purple, but is poisonous if swallowed. So work with it carefully. (The stains that it leaves on your skin will wear off in time but keep it off your clothes). Put a handful of berries in a

52. Plants that make good colors for paints

Wild grapes   Pokeberries

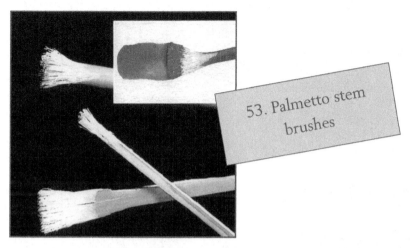

53. Palmetto stem brushes

handkerchief-sized piece of cloth and twist until the juice runs out. The juice of wild grapes is red. Adding a little powdered lime to the grape juice makes blue. Other berries that work are mulberries and blackberries. Experiment!

Mix the plant juice half-and-half with latex. Mix the dry powders with latex and add water until the paint goes on well. You can make brushes from split palmetto stems by chewing the ends to loosen the fibers (picture 53).

Picture 54 shows a couple of masks that my friends and I carved from soft wood and painted like masks made by the Calusa Indians hundreds of years ago at Key Marco.

The Calusa often painted designs on boards (see picture 55). Sometimes the boards were carved into shapes that meant something to the Calusa, but we have no idea what that was.

54. Masks we carved and painted

55. Calusa tablet

56. Calusa designs

57. Apalachee designs

If you would like to try using your paint the way these ancient people did, choose a light-colored board about five by eight inches in size. Apply your paints with the palmetto stem brushes and give the paint an hour or two to dry before putting on another color. Pictures 56 and 57 show some of the designs used by the Calusa who lived on Florida's Gulf coast and some used by the Apalachee who lived in the Panhandle.

7. MAKING FIRE

My friend John Beriault, an archaeologist who lives in Naples, told me a sad tale of a handful of archaeological finds rescued while the owner of a plant nursery was digging a pond. In the piles of draining muck brought up by a dragline were well preserved human bones plus carved bone and wood. The land belonged to the nurseryman and there were no laws to make him stop and allow a proper study of what was coming out of the pond. All John could do was to put together a team of people who scrambled over the soggy piles while the dragline kept digging. They were able to salvage only a little. The human remains turned out to be 6,700 years old. This site would have been another Windover!

Among the finds were small boards with a pattern of notches and holes. An archaeologist knows right away that these are fireboards. I will tell you about fireboards and how I learned to make fire the same way Florida people were doing it 6,000 years ago.

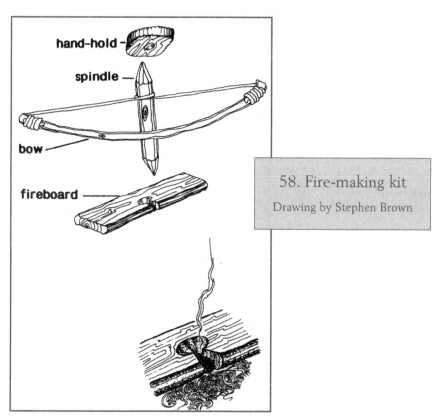

hand-hold

spindle

bow

fireboard

58. Fire-making kit

Drawing by Stephen Brown

Be careful of fire! This is a craft that an adult should help you learn. Keep the fire small and have a bucket of water nearby to keep the fire controlled and to soak it when you are through.

Remember always that the wood that you use must be really dry.

There are four parts to this Indian fire kit: handhold, spindle, fireboard, and bow. The **spindle** is ¾ inch in diameter, 8 inches long and pointed at both ends. Use a soft wood like cypress, willow, or fir. Don't use resinous wood like pine. Carve a point on both ends. The spindle works best if it is not perfectly round. Four or five flat areas on the spindle help the cord of the bow grip tightly and turn the spindle fast. The hearth or **fireboard** is the piece of wood in which the spindle turns. Friction between the spindle and the fireboard is what makes the fire. The fireboard should also be of soft wood, about 12 inches long, 3 inches wide, and ¾ inch thick. A third piece of wood, the **handhold**, is about

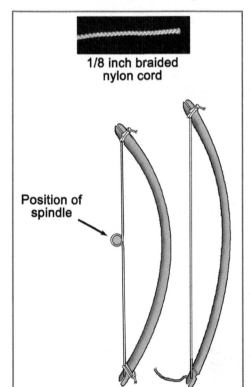

1/8 inch braided
nylon cord

Position of
spindle

59. Making the bow

3 inches square and 1 inch thick. It holds the top of the spindle and is best made of a hard wood like oak. About ¼ inch from one edge of the fireboard, carve a small cone-shaped hole into, but not all the way through it. (See picture 44 in chapter 5.) Do the same in the center of the handhold. The holes will hold the upper and lower ends of the spindle.

The **bow** is made from any springy wood—a willow branch works well—and should be about two feet long. The string for this bow has to be really tough. Indians probably used a narrow strip of rawhide, but you can use nylon cord. In each end of the bow, cut notches and a

IF YOU CAN'T GO NATURAL...
Even though it isn't real Indian stuff, ⅛ inch braided nylon cord from the hardware store is what you should use for your bow.

groove for the nylon cord as shown in picture 59. Put one end of the string into each notch. Tie one end and pull the bowstring through the notch in the other end just enough to bend the bow a little. Then tie off that end. Some oil on the handhold-end of the spindle keeps it from

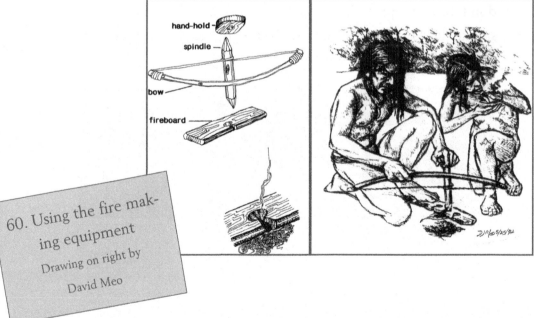

hand-hold
spindle
bow
fireboard

60. Using the fire mak-
ing equipment
Drawing on right by
David Meo

heating up and makes it spin better, so rub one end of the spindle on your face to get it a little oily. Always keep this oiled end—held by the handhold—up. If oil gets on the fireboard you won't have enough friction to make fire so mark the spindle by cutting a groove around the oiled end. In use, the spindle is on the outside of the bow as shown in the picture.

Have some fine splinters of dry wood or a small pile of pine needles ready to receive the fire.

Kneeling, hold the fireboard down with your left foot if you are right-handed. The left hand holds the handhold, and the right hand moves the bow back and forth, making the spindle spin in the shallow hole in the fireboard. Bow back and forth gently until you see smoke coming from the fireboard. You are making a black powder that is charcoal, and this is the stuff that will catch fire when you are bowing fast enough. Now cut a notch from the edge of the fireboard into the hole.

The stuff that will catch fire from the burning charcoal is called **tinder**. The fine reddish fibers from the trunk of a sabal palm or the fuzzy outer bark of the cedar tree make good tinder. Put some tinder beneath the notch in the fireboard. Kneeling in the same position, move the bow back and forth smoothly. You don't have to press hard on the handhold. Keep bowing until smoke starts coming from the fireboard and you can see finely powdered charcoal in the notch.

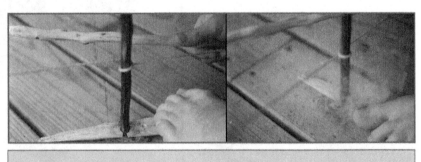

61. Bowing

62. Tinder catching fire

Keep bowing smoothly until the fireboard is putting out a lot of smoke.

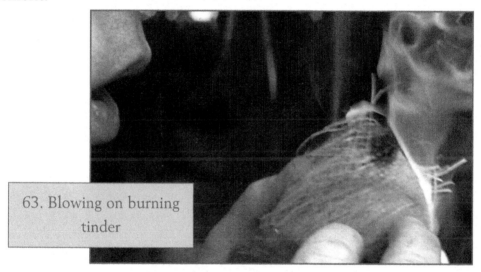

63. Blowing on burning tinder

Then lay the bow and spindle aside and lift up the fireboard and gently blow on the tinder that was under the fireboard. There should be a glowing bit of charcoal on the tinder. If there is, pick up the tinder and fold it around the glowing charcoal.

Gently blow on the burning charcoal until the tinder catches fire, then drop the burning tinder on the wood you have ready for the fire. Sometimes the glowing charcoal stays with the fireboard as you lift it. If it does, gently tap the fireboard over the tinder to drop the burning charcoal into the tinder.

The bowstring works best low on the spindle, close to the fireboard, but if it gets too close it can slip off the end of the spindle.

Timing is also important: too little bowing won't light the charcoal powder; too much bowing makes the spindle too blunt to build up heat. Blowing on the glowing charcoal to spread the fire to the tinder must be done gently. Be sure all parts are very dry.

Some Indian tribes made a "new fire" once a year and believed that the fire had magical powers. When you have made a fire without matches you will understand why the Indians felt that fire is something special! It takes more practice than strength, but it is not easy. Don't give up if you don't get fire the first time—or even the fifth time. But it is a neat trick, so practice!

8. HOLLOWING BY BURNING

One day, during my "how did they do it?" tries, I was sitting on a big stone in a creek near my home. I was working on a wooden bowl. Wooden bowls were used a lot by Florida's first people. They were usually made from a soft wood that carves easily like cypress. Quite a few bowls were found at Key Marco and most of them were very well made. I thought that the outside of the bowls was probably shaped by cutting and scraping with tools made of stone or shell. With a lot of work I roughed out an oval bowl from cypress wood and smoothed the outside by rubbing it on the stone that I was sitting on. When I tried digging out the wood to hollow the bowl, I had trouble. Scraping the wood out fiber-by-fiber was really slow. After two hours, I was covered with sweat and the bowl hadn't changed much. I gave up.

65. Calusa bowl made of Cypress
Courtesy Florida Museum of
Natural History

64. Hollowing out a spoon

For days I wondered how Florida's first people had made bowls. I knew that many Indians had made dugout canoes, and in Florida the

66. Starting the bowl

canoes weren't really dug out, but hollowed out by fire. Maybe fire would hollow out a bowl. I started looking through *The Bulletin of Primitive Technology,* and sure enough, there were pictures of burning the insides out of wooden bowls. The trick was to keep the fire burning in the right places by blowing on it. When the fire spread to the wrong places, it was put out by wetting the wood. Great! Here's how to do it:

Start with a soft wood like fir, basswood, or cypress. The solid piece should be 4 or 5 inches high, 4 or 5 inches long and 3 or 4 inches wide. The outside should be rounded but have a flat top (where you will begin the burning). The wood should by dry.

Make a pair of tongs for picking up the small pieces of burning wood. Take an 18-inch length of springy green wood like willow and bend it double in the middle. Tie the top of the legs of the tongs with a strip of willow bark so that the ends of the tongs stay about ¾ inch apart.

Make a blowpipe to keep the burning going. Use a piece of bamboo about ½ inch in diameter or a hollow stem like elder. The blowpipe should be 10 to 12 inches long so that you don't get too much smoke in your face.

You also need a bucket of water and some green Spanish moss. You will use the wet moss to dab water on the fire that is burning where you don't want it. Again, be careful of fire! Have an adult with you and work on a fireproof surface like a sidewalk or driveway.

67. Finishing the burning

Build a small fire on a concrete surface or in the family barbecue grill. Let it burn down to glowing pieces called coals. With the tongs, carefully pick up a glowing coal and place it on the flat surface of your bowl block where the hollow is to be. Blow gently on the coal using the blowpipe. The coal will begin to burn into the flat surface of your bowl.

The fire can be moved around by moving the coal to different places. Once you have burned a little hollow in your bowl, you can roll the coal to a different area to be burned. As long as the coal gets air, the wood beneath it will glow. Blow on it with the blowpipe to keep it glowing. Add more coals as needed.

Control the burning by dabbing with wet Spanish moss. From time to time check how deep the burn is going by scraping away the charcoal with a piece of stone or shell. When the inside of the bowl is large enough to suit you, drown the fire and scrape away the last of the black charcoal from the inside surface.

9. MAKING AND FIRING POTS

A few years ago I was back at the Florida Natural History Museum in Gainesville. This time I was in the ceramics lab of the Archaeology Department with Ann Cordell, the museum's expert on Florida Indian pottery. Clay pots that were being glued back into their original form and pieces of pottery covered her lab tables. By my chair was a stack of papers that Ann had copied for me. They were about making clay pots and what could be learned from ancient pieces of pottery.

68. Fired bowls

Ann said that about 4,000 years ago, a new craft appeared. Florida's first people learned that when dried clay is heated in a fire, it changes from a crumbly stuff that gets soft in water to a hard and lasting pottery that will hold water and that you can cook in. All over Florida, Indian potters began making things out of clay and heating them in a fire to make them strong. Things made from fire-hardened clay are called ceramics. At first the work of Florida Indians was pretty crude, but with time, potters became good at making both useful and beautiful things from clay—bowls, pots, plates, jars with lids, and pipes for smoking. Almost all of these things were made by coiling ropes of clay to make the hollow shape, then carefully smoothing the coils together. Florida Indian ceramics were not baked in an oven, but heated in an open fire.

After Florida's first people learned to make pottery, gathering, storing, and cooking were never the same again. And a new art was born.

The shapes of the pottery and the designs on it changed over the years, and archaeologists can often look at a broken piece of pottery (called a potsherd) and tell when and where it was made. Another very good thing about fired clay is that it lasts. Pottery that was made 4,000 years ago still shows the shape and decorations it had when it left the potter's hand. I had to try this craft.

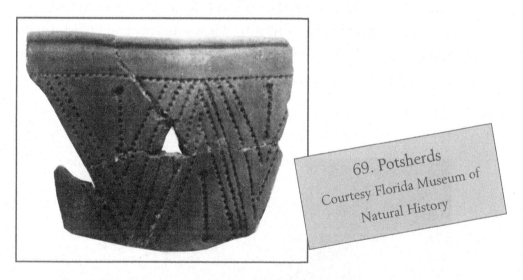

69. Potsherds
Courtesy Florida Museum of
Natural History

First, you need the right clay. Clay can be found all over Florida. Good clay feels squishy and sticky, but not sandy. If you want to dig your own clay, the best places to look are along the banks of streams and rivers and at cuts in the earth where roads go through hills. When you find stuff that looks like clay, you need to test it to see if it's useable. Roll out a clay rope about ¼ inch in diameter and three inches long. Coil it into a ring and stand the ring on its side. If the clay doesn't crack much when coiled and doesn't slump much when set on end, it probably can be made into ceramics.

You also need to know if the clay will stand firing—heating in a fire. Make a simple bowl about 1½ inch in diameter and let it dry for three days. Then test fire it by building a small fire around it or put it in with the charcoal when your family has a cookout. After about two hours in the fire, let your bowl cool slowly. It should be hard and it shouldn't soften in water. If the clay passes these tests, get a shovel and dig plenty of it. Pick out leaves, twigs, and rocks.

Stuff called temper must now be added to the clay to keep it from cracking when the pots are drying and when they are in the fire. The temper that Florida Indians usually used was sand. You can use sand from the beach. Mix 5 cups of clay with one cup of clean sand. Mash the sand into the clay and add a little water to make the sand and clay easier to work with. Then squeeze it and twist it until the two are mixed really well. This mixing has to be done right, so keep squeezing and twisting for about 20 minutes.

70. Mixing the sand and clay

Start your pot's bottom with a disk of clay about three inches in diameter and ¼ inch thick. Then roll out a few clay ropes that are about ¼ inch in diameter and six or eight inches long. Coil a rope upward from the edge of the disk to form the sides of the pot. Add coils one at a time and smooth each one into the coils below. After adding a few coils, you may need to keep one hand inside the pot

IF YOU CAN'T GO NATURAL...

If you can't find clay to use, you can buy clay at a craft supply store. The best kind is called raku clay, which works well in an open fire. If you don't live near the beach, you can get sand at a builder's supply or hardware store.

to hold up the wall as you blend in more coils. When the wall starts to slump or bend from the weight of the coils, set the pot in the shade to dry a little before doing any more work on it.

71. Beginning the pot

Start a new pot while the first one dries. Work on two or three pots at a time so that one is always stiff enough to let you add more coils. Stop when the pot is four or five inches high. With moist fingers, smooth the pot all over.

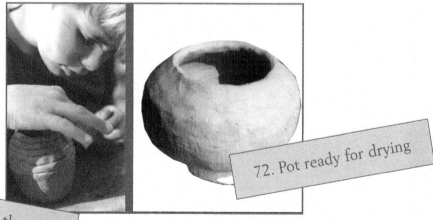

72. Pot ready for drying

72. Smoothing the coils

While the pot is still a little wet, you can add a design by punching dots or scratching lines with a small stick. The Indians made a lot of deep bowls with a design of crisscrossed lines on them. The design's rough surface made it easier to hold on to the bowl.

73. A Weeden Island pot

About 1,600 years ago Florida native potters of the Weeden Island period made ceramics of great beauty. Look closely at the pictures of their pottery (73 and 74).

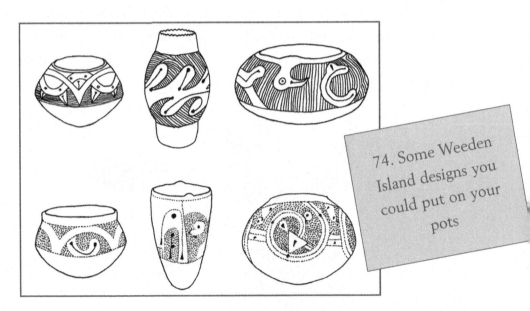

74. Some Weeden Island designs you could put on your pots

Let your pots dry in the shade for a week. Drying too fast can make cracks. When they are dry, try polishing the outside of a pot with a smooth stone. This is called **burnishing**. It is slow work, but burnishing can make a nice shiny surface that looks like the pot is glazed. Florida's Indian potters were very good at burnishing, but they never learned to make a true glaze for their pots. If you have found clay of a different color from the clay that you used to make your pot, you can use it for decoration. Make it into a thick paint by adding water to a little clay. Make a brush by chewing the end of a twig or a piece of palmetto stem and paint a design on your pots. A special kind of Florida pottery with painted red clay designs is called Dunn's Creek Red. It was named for the creek where it was first found.

75. Pots ready to fire

When the pots are dry, you are ready to harden them in fire. This time you are going to make a big fire, so do this with an adult and have the garden hose hooked up and close to the fire site. Don't burn when things are so dry that the forestry service forbids open fires, and don't burn on a very windy day. Wetting the pots while they are in the fire will crack them so don't burn when rain is predicted. Choose an open area with no overhanging trees. Rake away leaves or pine needles—anything that might burn—from an area about 30 feet in diameter. Lay down a few flat stones to make a platform that will keep your pots off the ground and place the pots upside down on the stone platform.

Protect the pots by covering them with pieces of broken pottery—old flower pots work well. Gather plenty of dry wood and pile it 30 feet away from the fire site. Pine needles and pinecones are good starters. Twigs and dry branches two to three feet long are good for keeping the fire going. You will need a lot!

Place a ring of dry pine needles and cones on the ground around the stacked pots, about three feet out from them.

Light this ring in two or three places and keep it burning by adding twigs and pinecones. This warms the pots and drives out

76. Beginning the firing

77. Firing

the last of the water held in the clay. Keep the ring of fire burning for an hour. Then add larger branches to the ring of fire, slowly moving the fire inward toward the pots. After about half an hour the fire should be right up to the pots. Gently prop large branches over the heated pots until the fire is really hot and covers the pots completely. Keep this hot fire burning for about two hours.

78. Cooling

Let the fire die, but don't try to remove the pots from the ashes until they are cool. Since you can't put this fire out with water, watch the fire until the last coals have died. Starting the firing in the early afternoon lets you watch the last glowing coals as night falls and you can see them better. When the pots are cool enough to touch, (usually the next morning), lift them from the ashes. Don't be surprised if some of your work has cracks. Indian potters also lost a lot of pots in the firing.

The color of the clay will be different after firing. Most colors are brighter and some clays turn orange or red. If there were places in the fire that didn't get oxygen, you will see dark areas called fire clouds on your pots.

79. Some finished pots

IF YOU CAN'T GO NATURAL...

If you can't do an open firing, your pots can be baked in a special oven called a kiln. You will have to find a local potter who will let you use his or her kiln.

LEARNING MORE

ere are some ways that you can learn more about Indian crafts and about Florida's first people.

GENERAL TOPICS

Florida's First People by Robin Brown. 1994. Pineapple Press.

The Southeastern Indians by Charles Hudson. 1976. The University of Tennessee Press.

Native Americans in Florida by Kevin McCarthy. 1999. Pineapple Press

The Indians of Florida by Jerald Milanich. 1998. University Press of Florida.

The Bulletin of Primitive Technology. Join The Society of Primitive Technology for $20.00 a year and get *The Bulletin of Primitive Technology*, an excellent magazine, sent to you twice a year. The address is: P.O. Box 905, Rexburg ID 83440.

You can also get articles from back issues of the *Bulletin* from your local public library. Many good articles are listed with each craft below. Show the librarian the issue number, date, and page (all are listed below) of the article you want and ask to get it on interlibrary loan.

CORD, STRING, AND ROPE

Indian Fishing: Early Methods on the Northwest Coast by Hilary Stewart. 1977. University of Washington Press.

The Material Culture of Key Marco by Marion Gilliland. 1975. The University Press of Florida.

"Plant Fiber Preparation" by David Westcott and John McPherson in *The Bulletin of Primitive Technology*, Fall 1991, Number 2 , pages 12–15.

"Cordage" by Steven Edholm and Tamara Wilder in *The Bulletin of Primitive Technology*, Fall 1991, Number 2, pages 19–20.

"The Basswood" by Phillip D. Moore in *The Bulletin of Primitive Technology*, Fall 1991, Number 2, pages 21–24.

"Making Cordage by Hand" by Norm Kidder in *The Bulletin of Primitive Technology*, Fall 1996, Number 12, pages 42–45.

WEAVING

Wet Site Archaeology edited by Barbara Purdy. 1988. The University Press of Florida. pages 263–291.

"A Simple Weaving Technique" by John Leeds in *The Bulletin of Primitive Technology*, Fall 1998, Number 16, pages 55–58.

BASKET MAKING

Natural Basketry by Carol Hart. 1976. Watson Gluptill Publications.

"Palmetto Hat" by Ray Bornstein in *The Bulletin of Primitive Technology*, Fall 1994, Number 8, page 27.

TRAPS

Indians by Edwin Tunis. 1979. Thomas Crowell Press.

"'Rocking On' with the Paiute Deadfall" by Jim Riggs in *The Bulletin of Primitive Technology*, Spring 1992, Number 3, pages 38–46.

"Trapping: Take a New Look" by Matt McMahon in *The Bulletin of Primitive Technology*, Spring 1992, Number 3, pages 48–51.

"The Sampson Deadfall" by James Andal in *The Bulletin of Primitive Technology*, Fall 1994, Number 8, page 68.

ATLATLS

"Great Basin Atlatls" by Steve Alley in *The Bulletin of Primitive Technology*, Fall 1992, Number 4, pages 48–56.

"Reconstructing the Generic Basketmaker Atlatl" by Wryley Hunter in *The Bulletin of Primitive Technology*, Fall 1992, Number 4, pages 57–61.

"The Tuning of Atlatl Darts" by Richard A. Baugh in *The Bulletin of Primitive Technology*, Spring 2002, Number 23, pages 89–91.

"Atlatl Spurs" by Ray Strischek in *The Bulletin of Primitive Technology*, Fall 1999, Number 18, pages 70–73.

"Atlatls: Throwing for Distance" by Craig Ratzat in *The Bulletin of Primitive Technology*, Fall 1992, Number 4, pages 62–63.

PAINTS

Exploration of the Ancient Key Dwellers' Remains on the Gulf Coast of Florida by Frank Hamilton Cushing. Written 1898. Publlished by The University Press of Florida in 1998.

MAKING FIRE

Tom Brown's Guide to Nature and Survival by Tom Brown Jr. 1989. Berkeley Books.

"The Hand-drilled Fire" by William McPherson in *The Bulletin of Primitive Technology*, Spring 1991, Number 1, pages 16–18.

"Neophytic Notes on Fire Making with Friction" by R. Alan Mountier in *The Bulletin of Primitive Technology*, Fall 1999, Number 18, Pages 49–57.

"Friction Fire for the Downhearted" by Jim Allen in *The Bulletin of Primitive Technology*, Fall 1999, Number 18, pages 58–59.

"Bow Drill Fire-Making for Young Kids" by Robin Moore in *The Bulletin of Primitive Technology*, Spring 1995, Number 11, page 27.

"Tinder Bundle" by Charles Worsham in *The Bulletin of Primitive Technology*, Fall 1994, Number 8, pages 81–83.

HOLLOWING BY BURNING

"The Amazing Coal Burned Spoon" by Ricardo Sierra in *The Bulletin of Primitive Technology*, Spring 1995, Number 11, page 41.

MAKING AND FIRING POTS

Pottery Analysis by Prudence Rice. 1987. University of Chicago Press.

"Primitive Pottery Firing" by Maria-Louise Sideroff in *The Bulletin of Primitive Technology*, Fall 1991, Number 2, pages 58–59.

"A Sure-Fire Way to Fire Pots" by Kohn Olsen in *The Bulletin of Primitive Technology*, Spring 1998, Number 15, pages 34–36

"Kids and Clay" by Jeff Gottlieb in *The Bulletin of Primitive Technology*, Spring 1998, Number 15, Page 57.

"What's the Color of Your Clay?" by Maria Sideroff in *The Bulletin of Primitive Technology*, Spring 1991, Number 1, pages 29–32.

"Introduction to Ceramic Replication" by Maria Sideroff in *The Bulletin of Primitive Technology*, Spring 1991, Number 1, pages 27–29.

Here are some other books from Pineapple Press that might interest you. For a complete catalog, write to Pineapple Press, P.O. Box 3889, Sarasota, Florida 34230-3889, or call (800) 746-3275. Or visit our website at www.pineapplepress.com.

Patchwork by Dorothy Downs. A hands-on way to learn about Florida's Seminoles and Miccosukees, who have been making and wearing patchwork clothing since the early 1900s. Ages 9–12.

Native Americans in Florida by Kevin McCarthy. Teaches about the many diverse Indian tribes in Florida from prehistoric times to the present. Includes information about archaeology, an extensive glossary, and legends that teach moral lessons. A teacher's manual is also available. All ages.

Legends of the Seminoles by Betty Mae Jumper. This collection of rich, spoken tales—written down for the first time—impart valuable lessons about living in harmony with nature and about why the world is the way it is. Each story is illustrated with an original color painting. All ages.

Florida's First People by Robin Brown. Filled with photos of replicas of the technologies used by early peoples in their daily lives, this book brings to life the first humans who lived in Florida about 12,000 years ago. Great for a budding archaeologist or historian. All ages.

Florida's Fossils by Robin Brown. Includes a complete identification section and insightful comments on the history of the fossil treasures you'll uncover. Amateur archaeologists will appreciate updated maps and directions to some of the best fossil-hunting sites in Florida. All ages.

Ice Age Giants of the South by Judy Cutchins and Ginny Johnston. First in the Southern Fossil Discoveries series, this full-color book chronicles up-to-date discoveries in the field of archaeology and describes how prehistoric animals looked, how they lived, and what they ate. Ages 8–12.

Giant Predators of the Ancient Seas by Judy Cutchins and Ginny Johnston. Second in the Southern Fossil Discoveries series, this full-color book explores how scientists use fossil clues to learn about the lives and habitats of the most exciting sea animals that ever lived. Ages 8–12.

Dinosaurs of the South by Judy Cutchins and Ginny Johnston. Third in the Southern Fossil Discoveries series, this full-color book uncovers the variety of dinosaurs and giant reptiles that once lived in Southern forests and coastal lowlands. Ages 8–12.

America's REAL First Thanksgiving by Robyn Gioia. Fifty-six years before the Pilgrims landed in New England, Spanish explorer Menendez founded the first North American city, St. Augustine. The Spanish celebrated a thanksgiving meal with the Florida natives. Learn how to make the food they likely ate that day. Ages 9–14.